LAURA INGALLS WILDER COUNTRY

Text by
WILLIAM ANDERSON

Color Photography by
LESLIE A. KELLY

HarperPerennial
A Division of HarperCollinsPublishers

An edition of this book was published in Japan by Kyuryudo Art Publishing in 1988.

LAURA INGALLS WILDER COUNTRY. Copyright © 1990 by William Anderson. Color photographs copyright © 1988, 1990 by Leslie A. Kelly. Illustrations copyright © 1953, 1971 by Garth Williams. All rights reserved. Printed in the United States of America. No part of this book may be used or reproduced in any manner whatsoever without written permission except in the case of brief quotations embodied in critical articles and reviews. For information address HarperCollins Publishers, 10 East 53rd Street, New York, NY 10022.

FIRST EDITION

Library of Congress Cataloging-in-Publication Data
Anderson, William, 1952–
    Laura Ingalls Wilder country / William Anderson. — 1st
HarperPerennial ed.
        p.   cm.
    "Originally published by Kyuryudo Art Publishing of Tokyo, Japan"—
T.p. verso.
    ISBN 0-06-055294-8 (cloth) — ISBN 0-06-097346-3 (pbk.)
    1. Wilder, Laura Ingalls, 1867–1957—Homes and haunts.
2. Authors, American—20th century—Biography.   3. Frontier and
pioneer life—United States.   4. Literary landmarks—United States.
I. Title.
PS3545.I342Z557   1990
813'.52—dc20
[B]
                                                          89-46512
90 91 92 93 94 CC/RA 10 9 8 7 6 5 4 3 2 1

90 91 92 93 94 CC/RA 10 9 8 7 6 5 4 3 2 1 (pbk.)

Contents

Preface

Laura Ingalls Wilder Country is the result of a series of happy coincidences, a combination of talents, and an international interest in the Little House books about American pioneering. This photographic book was unofficially born at the Laura Ingalls Wilder Room of the Pomona Public Library in California on February 7, 1987, the 120th anniversary of Laura Ingalls Wilder's birth.

For West Coast Little House readers, the Pomona Public Library has hosted an annual gathering on February 7 ever since the dedication of the Laura Ingalls Wilder Room in 1950. I was a guest and speaker at the 1987 observance.

Among the hundreds of enthusiasts who flocked into the Wilder Room that February 7 was a camera-toting father of two, Leslie A. Kelly. I noticed his camera flashing over the array of children dressed in pioneer costumes, the displays of Laura's manuscripts, and the huge birthday cake shaped like a log cabin—and an idea clicked with me.

At home on my desk in Michigan was a letter from a Japanese translator, Yumiko Taniguchi. Her Little House book translations and her admiration for the Wilder writings helped introduce Laura Ingalls Wilder to Japan. Because of the great interest among the Japanese readers, Yumiko longed to see a book published depicting the land and places

Laura described in her books. Most Japanese readers had never seen the rural beauty of the Ingalls and Wilder homesites on the wide prairies and in the dense forests. Yumiko asked me to describe those places in words, based on my long familiarity with them. But the words needed more than the images they suggested. A photographer was essential to the project, to capture those wide sweeps of endless plains, that blue-bowl sky overhead, and all that lay between.

When I asked Les Kelly if he would photograph Wilder country, he agreed with the eagerness of any pioneer. He was well versed in the lore and the legend from many readings of the Little House books in his home with his children Erin and Patrick. Ultimately, he made four journeys to the Midwest heartland to capture the remaining authentic homes, the established museums, and the carefully kept artifacts of the type known to Laura Ingalls Wilder. For this book, he has gathered the most important aspects of what remains from Laura's past and what is preserved for the future.

In De Smet, South Dakota, the kindness of Vivian Glover, director of the Laura Ingalls Wilder Memorial Society, opened the doors of the two restored Ingalls homes. Long photo sessions lasted late into the night as Les recorded the rooms and relics carefully tended to in the Ingalls House and the Surveyors' House. Half a year later, when a blizzard blasted over the prairie, rivaling any experienced during the hard winter of 1880–1881, Vivian accompanied Les in a sturdy four-wheel-drive vehicle to photograph frosted cottonwoods, frozen flat lands, and a ghostly, icy white mist that formed over the land.

In Walnut Grove, Minnesota, the hospitality of Shirley Knakmuhs of the Laura Ingalls Wilder Museum and Visitor Center helped add to the growing collection of scenes familiar from Laura's prose.

The late Fern Marcks of the Laura Ingalls Wilder Society of Pepin, Wisconsin, hosted Les Kelly as he photographed the big lake, the Big Woods, and vicinity. At Burr Oak, Iowa, Evelyn Underbakke was tour director at the restored hotel once operated by the Ingalls family.

In Independence, Kansas, Les was guided over the former Osage Indian hunting grounds by the current owners of the *Little House on the Prairie* site, General Bill and Wilma Kurtis.

Through the courtesy of the Laura Ingalls Wilder Home Association of Mansfield, Missouri, the house on Rocky Ridge Farm was opened for the first time for extensive photography. The Les Kelly photographs of the rustic rooms with their well-worn furniture and odd nooks and niches vividly depict the independent, individualistic lives of Laura and Almanzo Wilder as Ozark farmers.

Laura Ingalls Wilder Country was designed by Yumiko Taniguchi and first published in 1988 by the Kyuryudo Art Publishing Company, Ltd. The book's impact was so great in Japan that it prompted a touring Laura Ingalls Wilder Exhibition in 1989. This exhibit marked the first international showing of original artifacts and treasures from the Rocky Ridge farmhouse, loaned by the Laura Ingalls Wilder Home Association.

"The land you couldn't see to the end of" is the way Laura Ingalls Wilder described her Midwest of the 1870s and 1880s. In these pages, that land and the life of the pioneer author live again for her American family of readers.

William Anderson

William Anderson
June 25, 1990

Introduction

When Laura Ingalls Wilder started publishing her series of Little House books in 1932, she had no idea that she was creating a lasting fame for herself and the places she had lived. She wrote simply to preserve what she considered a good story, the saga of her family's struggles and joys as they pioneered in the woodlands and prairies of frontier America during the 1870s and 1880s.

"These were family stories and I believed that they should be preserved," Laura explained. "They were altogether too good to be lost." Her first book, *Little House in the Big Woods,* was published when she was sixty-five. It was tremendously popular with readers and was followed by six more volumes in which Laura described her life as a pioneer girl and *Farmer Boy,* the story of her husband, Almanzo Wilder.

Laura's eight-volume Little House series kept her busily writing through the 1930s and 1940s because readers "would not allow me to stop." The series included *Little House in the Big Woods, Farmer Boy, Little House on the Prairie, On the Banks of Plum Creek, By the Shores of Silver Lake, The Long Winter, Little Town on the Prairie,* and *These Happy Golden Years.* * Perhaps the most famous book is *Little House on the Prairie,* which became the basis for the long-running television series of the same name. All of the Little House books have been translated into scores of languages.

Following Laura's death in 1957, after a hearty ninety years, two additional books were added to her classic series. *On the Way Home* was published by her writer-daughter, Rose Wilder Lane, in 1962. In 1971, *The First Four Years* appeared; it had been discovered in manuscript form among Laura's lifetime collection of papers, rough drafts, letters, and manuscripts.

Laura Ingalls Wilder lived to see her books read and enjoyed by admirers all over the world. "It is a continual pleasure to me to know that my books are read," she often remarked. When asked to explain the popularity of her writing, Laura could not perceive herself as a talented author. She modestly suggested that perhaps readers enjoyed her books because they were about real people and actual places.

They were. Laura's own family provided the characters who peopled her stories, and her husband, Almanzo Wilder, was the hero of the final four volumes. The places where the Ingalls and Wilder families settled were authentic locales scattered across the broad heartland of America.

"The Big Woods," where Laura was born and where she began her story settings, was near Pepin,

---

*All published by Harper & Row.

Wisconsin. "Indian Territory," where the Ingalls family first pioneered, was near Independence, Kansas. "Plum Creek" flowed through Walnut Grove, Minnesota. Laura's "little town on the prairie" was De Smet, South Dakota. Almanzo Wilder, the "farmer boy," grew up near Malone, New York. Only two years of Laura's girlhood were left out of her autobiographical narrative. The Ingalls family spent that interlude operating a frontier hotel at Burr Oak, Iowa.

In 1894, nine years after their marriage, Laura and Almanzo, with their seven-year-old daughter Rose, settled in the Ozark Mountains near Mansfield, Missouri. Laura and Almanzo moved no more, content to farm among the green valleys of southern Missouri.

During Laura's late-life fame as a writer, her readers continually sought her out in the Missouri farmhouse where she lived for sixty years. With her directions, many went on to trace the trail to all her book sites. They still do.

Each of Laura's hometowns now honors her. Some of the "little houses" she wrote about still exist. All of the Little House sites proudly maintain museums, preserved houses, and landmarks in tribute to Laura Ingalls Wilder.

Each summer, Little House readers stream through the doors of a Wisconsin log cabin, the house in De Smet, and the farmhouse in Mansfield. Plays and pageants are produced on the same prairie lands where Laura Ingalls once walked. Treasured mementoes and artifacts are preserved at each of the book sites, reflecting the reality of Laura's painstakingly written stories.

The story continues as readers discover both the Little House books and the places where they took place. For those who love Laura, this book will shed light on her long-ago life during the exciting pioneering era of America's past.

LAURA INGALLS WILDER COUNTRY

CHAPTER 1

The Big Woods of Wisconsin

For Laura Elizabeth Ingalls, the tall trees of the Big Woods of Wisconsin and a snug log cabin in a clearing were the first memories of the world surrounding her. She was born on February 7, 1867, in the home created by her parents, Charles and Caroline Ingalls. There she began her lifelong practice of preserving her experiences with the written word.

In 1932, sixty-five years after her birth in that cabin in the woods, Laura Ingalls Wilder published her first book, *Little House in the Big Woods.* When the book appeared, the tale of Laura's Pa and Ma and her sister, Mary, and their pioneer home near Pepin, Wisconsin, seemed to reflect a long-lost period of American history. To Laura, her memories were "stories that had to be told." She claimed that she "wanted children to understand more about the beginnings of things—what it is that made America."

"Children today," Laura said, "could not have a childhood like mine in the Big Woods of Wisconsin, but they could learn of it and hear the stories that Pa used to tell. Oh yes! The pictures that hang in my memory. The first sign of approaching old age has come to me, for I love to look back on them." For Laura, looking back on her recollections also meant writing them.

Happiest among Laura's memories were the long winter evenings in the log cabin with Pa and Ma and her sisters. The warm fire flickered in the fireplace, the day's work was complete, and best of all, Pa played his fiddle and told stories.

As Laura wrote to her daughter, Rose,

> The evening storm winds howled outside
> The snow with darkness fell;
> And the firelight and the shadows,
> Wove many a magic spell,
> As I listened to the stories
> That Father used to tell.

The tall trees and endless forests of the Big Woods were cleared to create rolling farmland, but the site of Laura Ingalls Wilder's birthplace was located and marked by Pepin residents who were eager to pay tribute to their native author. In 1976, the Little House Wayside was created along Highway 183. A log cabin was constructed to serve as a reminder of the one that sheltered Pa and Ma and Mary and Laura in the 1860s.

Charles Ingalls, a renowned hunter, trapper, and woodsman, reveled in the thick Wisconsin forests that bordered his cabin in the clearing. "He was the swiftest skater in the neighborhood," Laura wrote, "[he was] a strong swimmer and could travel for miles on his snow shoes or tramp all day through the woods without fatigue. My first memory is of his eyes, so clear and sharp and blue. Those eyes . . . could look unerringly along a rifle barrel in the face of a bear or a pack of wolves and yet were so tender as they rested on his Caroline. . . ."

Around 1870, members of the Ingalls family gathered together for a portrait. Laura's grandparents, Laura and Lansford, are seated in the center, flanked by their daughters Lydia Louisa *(left)* and Ruby *(right)*. Standing, left to right, are Lansford James, George, and Hiram. Charles had already yielded to his keen desire to travel west when this picture was taken. These are the grandparents, aunts, and uncles Laura Ingalls Wilder described in *Little House in the Big Woods.*

Laura wrote, "Our little family must be self-sufficient for its own entertainment as well as its livelihood. Mother was descended from an old Scotch family and inherited the Scotch thriftiness. Although born and raised on the frontier she was an educated, cultured woman. Father was also raised on the frontier. He was always jolly, inclined to be reckless and loved his violin."

Although the Wisconsin woods were deep and dark, beauty lived there . . .

Black-eyed Susans bloomed in the summer . . .

Berries provided fruit, juice for ink, or a red mouth for a rag doll . . .

And Laura and Mary gathered wildflowers to make the log cabin pretty . . .

Down the road from the Ingalls cabin was the Barry Corner School for which Charles Ingalls was treasurer. Although she did not mention it in *Little House in the Big Woods,* Laura attended the school with Mary in 1871. At four, Laura was the youngest of all of Miss Anna Barry's pupils. It was in the Barry Corner School that Laura first cultivated her love of words, both reading and writing them.

Mary's patchwork quilt was made in the little house in the Big Woods, and is now on display at the Laura Ingalls Wilder Home and Museum in Mansfield, Missouri.

The Huleatt family, who lived on a farm called Oakland, were great friends of the Ingalls family. The Ingalls family photograph album is opened to pictures of Clarence and Eva Huleatt, Laura's first friends in Wisconsin.

22

Lake Pepin is an expansion of the Mississippi River, thirty miles long and three miles at its widest. The town of Pepin was first built along the lakeshore, and then extended up the bluffs that rise to the east. The site of *Little House in the Big Woods* was seven miles northwest of Pepin. Lake Pepin prompted many Indian legends and tales, and in the firelit evenings, Pa Ingalls repeated them to his girls.

Laura described her first visit to Pepin in *Little House in the Big Woods.*

Laura gathered so many pebbles from the shore of Lake Pepin that they tore the pocket from her dress.

The Pepin School, built in 1857, as Laura Ingalls knew it. At the close of the Civil War in 1865, Pepin held a Peace Celebration at the school.

CHAPTER 2

In the spring and summer, the prairies resembled an ever-changing array of wildflowers.

The Verdigris River flowed across the prairie at Independence. Though Laura recalled Pa's round-trips to town from their cabin as forty-mile journeys, the distance is actually less than fifteen miles from Independence to the home-site.

Kansas Prairie Country

In 1935, Laura Ingalls Wilder published *Little House on the Prairie.* Following the publication of her first book in 1932, she found that she "was not being allowed to stop." Children wrote letters begging for more stories of the Ingalls family. Laura then outlined her plan to write "an eight volume historical novel for children, covering every aspect of the American frontier."

Little House on the Prairie recounted the long covered-wagon journey which took the Ingalls family from their Wisconsin home across the Mississippi, through Minnesota, Iowa, Missouri, and into Kansas. Laura was two when they started the trek in 1869; much of her writing material was derived from stories she later heard of the long trip to the prairies.

Pa and Ma settled about thirteen miles south of the town of Independence, Kansas. Unwittingly, they had driven into the Osage Diminished Reserve, a corner of land set aside for the Indians. There they built their log cabin and Pa started to break the acres of virgin prairie with his plow.

Living on the prairie was endlessly interesting for Laura and Mary. Snakes, gophers, rabbits, birds, flowers, and insects lived in the tall, green grasses. Remembering her first sighting of a slithering garter snake, Laura wrote that "Ma said that little garter snakes were not poisonous and would not hurt us, but it was safer always to keep away from snakes."

Cattle graze on the peaceful prairie that was once hunting grounds for the Osage Indian tribes.

The original Ingalls cabin had disappeared by the time Laura started writing *Little House on the Prairie.* During her work on the book, Laura studied maps, researched historical records, and traveled with her daughter, Rose, to the vicinity she used as her book's setting.

Because of the fame of *Little House on the Prairie,* Kansans wanted to know where the Ingalls cabin had stood. An Independence, Kansas, bookseller, Margaret Clement, carefully researched old land records and clues in Laura's book. She consulted the 1870 census records and found the Ingalls family listed in Rutland Township, Montgomery County. Charles, Caroline, Mary, Laura, and a newborn baby, Caroline, were listed in

The well, which was dug with the help of Mr. Scott, the neighbor who traded work with Pa.

the August 1870 enumeration. Combining her data, Margaret Clement pinpointed the spot where the Ingalls had settled.

Foundation stones and a hand-dug pioneer well were located on the ranch of the William Kurtis family. An authentic replica of the cabin Pa built was constructed at the site.

The *Little House on the Prairie* site includes the former post office from Wayside, Kansas, and a typical one-room schoolhouse.

27

When the Ingalls family lived in Kansas, prairie chickens far outnumbered neighbors.

Pa exchanged work with other settlers; a family favorite was Mr. Edwards, who lived nearby. It was Mr. Edwards who brought Santa Claus's presents to Laura and Mary. He would walk to Independence to fetch the gifts and then swim the flooded Walnut Creek to deliver them.

"And there are more people around here than you'd think," Pa told Ma when he returned to the little cabin from one of his hunting trips. "Squatters are settling in the little valleys. I was at Scotts' place today. Nice folks. If we need anything badly, perhaps they could help us out." (unpublished passage from the first-draft manuscript of *Little House on the Prairie*)

The foundation remains of an old log cabin are believed to be the homesite of Mr. Edwards, the rawboned Tennessee bachelor who befriended the Ingallses.

28

Doctor George Tann, a black physician to the Indians and the pioneers, is mentioned in *Little House on the Prairie.* When the Ingalls family suffered with malaria (Laura called the disease "fever 'n ague"), Doctor Tann tended them faithfully. He is buried in Independence.

Laura saw Main Street in Independence, Kansas, several times. It was here that Pa traveled to trade his furs and buy supplies and tools while the family lived in the cabin on the prairie.

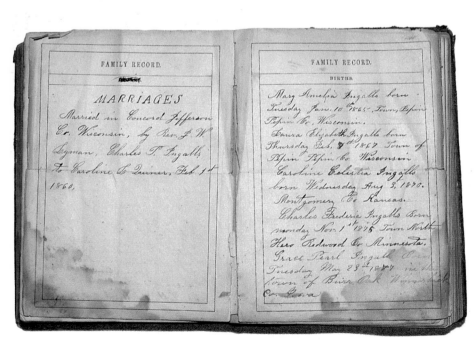

The Ingalls family Bible, now at the Laura Ingalls Wilder Home and Museum in Mansfield, Missouri, recorded the birth of Baby Carrie, on August 3, 1870. When Pa, Mary, and Laura returned from a day exploring an abandoned Indian camp, they discovered a new sister had been born.

Helen Sewell depicted Ma and the girls in the 1935 edition of *Little House on the Prairie.*

The Kansas prairie looked like a good place to settle, but it was Indian country. The Osage tribes worried that settlers would crowd them away and encroach upon their hunting grounds. All her life, Laura recalled the Indian war chants as the tribes concerned themselves with whether to drive away the settlers. Then Pa heard that the United States Army was riding in to drive off the settlers from the Indian domain. A letter had arrived from Wisconsin, stating that the man who had purchased the Pepin farm could not pay for it. Pa and Ma could take possession of their old home again. They decided to leave Kansas.

An Osage tribesman, circa 1870.

"In those days," Laura remarked, "once people started going West, they usually kept on going, making stops along the way."

CHAPTER 3

Walnut Grove and the Banks of Plum Creek

"Wisconsin is not so bad," Pa told the family. "There will be good fishing in Lake Pepin and hunting in the Big Woods. There'll be strawberries on the hill slopes—and sprouts in the wheat field, but what're a few sprouts?" The Ingalls family returned to their farm in the woods near Pepin in 1871. But Pa still longed for the West. For two years, while he farmed his Wisconsin land, Pa talked of going west again.

Ma laughed and said that Pa had an itchy foot. Early in the spring of 1873, after selling the farm a second time, the covered wagon was packed and the Ingalls family set out again. Pa's aim was to settle on the prairies of western Minnesota. Laura was six then, Mary was eight, and Carrie was almost three.

Each day, Pa's horses drew the wagon farther west. One night Pa and Ma camped in a creek bottom. Just as Laura was nearly asleep, she heard what she called "a clear, wonderful call." Ma told her it was a train whistle, going west. In the twilight, Laura watched the engine and the train, the first she had ever seen. She heard the puffing engine and the rattling cars on the tracks. She saw the lighted cars, with travelers seated inside, speeding through the dark. Pa told her that they were living in a great age and that railroads were conquering the frontier.

Like that speeding train, Laura faced West. She was a pioneer girl, a part of a great exodus of people and a part of progress. When Pa's covered wagon finally came to a stop along a creek bank near the pioneer village of Walnut Grove, Minnesota, Laura had completed just one in a long succession of moves with her frontier family.

Charles and Caroline Ingalls bought 172 acres of fertile prairie land in North Hero Township, Redwood County, Minnesota. Their farm was two miles north of Walnut Grove. Plum Creek flowed through the Ingalls homestead, and in its bank was a dugout that became their first home in Minnesota.

In November 1947, illustrator Garth Williams visited the Plum Creek site near Walnut Grove in preparation for a newly illustrated version of *On the Banks of Plum Creek.* Later he told Laura that "I wandered along the creek, with my camera and sketch-book, looking for a possible place for a sod-house in the bank."

Wild plums thrive near the creek.

The creek as it looked when Garth Williams photographed it in 1947. "It was most exciting," the artist told the author, "to sit on the bank and imagine the foot-bridge and you and Nellie Oleson splashing in the water."

The dugout remained intact for many years after the Ingalls family lived along Plum Creek. Finally, the sod roof collapsed and the walls dissolved back into the creek bank. Jane Myers, an early visitor to the site, wrote: "Floods have been here to wash away the dugout, leaving only a substantial dent in the bank. Wild roses bloomed here and wild white morning glories. The top of the steep bank waved high with timeless blowing grasses." (from Laura's unpublished autobiography, *Pioneer Girl*)

Wrote Laura: "A perfectly round tableland rose straight up on all sides, perhaps six feet above the lower ground. The sides were so steep that we could not climb straight up, but we had to go sideways up them. We pretended that this was our fort and that Indians were hiding in the plum trees along the creek."

When his wheat crop was planted, Pa was eager to move his family from the creek-bank dugout. On the opposite side of the creek, nearer to the road into Walnut Grove, Pa built their first house of sawed lumber. There were glass windows and factory-made doors with china doorknobs. And on moving day, Pa surprised Ma with a patented cookstove. Helen Sewell and Mildred Boyle depicted Ma's surprise in *On the Banks of Plum Creek.*

On the treeless prairies, pioneers often used sod to construct their shelters. Laura described the dugout along Plum Creek as "a funny little house to move into."

"It was not much bigger than the wagon," she wrote. "It had only one room, dug into the creek bank like a cave. Willows had been laid over it and grass sods laid on them; the grass grew tall and thick on this roof, which looked exactly like the rest of the prairie." (*Pioneer Girl*)

Harold and Della Gordon bought the Ingalls farmland in 1946, but they had no idea they were purchasing a piece of history. In 1953, Della Gordon wrote to Laura, telling her of the Plum Creek property as it was then.

"It was a lovely place," Laura replied, "and I often think of it even yet and of the happy times I had playing along and *in* the creek."

The frame house that Pa built near Plum Creek stood until the 1940s. When it was dismantled, lumber from what Laura called "the wonderful house" was used to construct this farm building.

Eleck and Olena Nelson and their children were the nearest neighbors the Ingalls had along Plum Creek. Eleck Nelson, a Norwegian immigrant, was the first settler to file a homestead claim on land in North Hero Township. Anna Nelson, mentioned in *On the Banks of Plum Creek,* stood between her parents for this family portrait.

Walnut Grove, Minnesota, as it looks today.

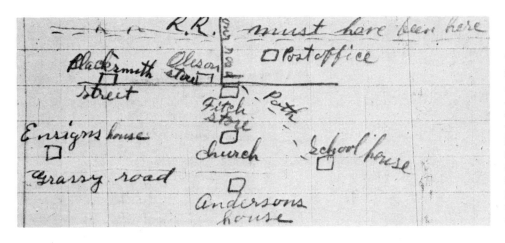

"Our farm was north of town and the road from it to town ran almost straight south . . . on section lines after it left our land. All roads went on section lines in prairie country. The street in town ran east and west, the church was south and the school house still farther south. . . . [Walnut Grove was] Just a little wide place beside the tracks." Laura's description of Walnut Grove as she remembered it in a letter to her daughter, Rose, was also accompanied with a map drawn to clarify details as she wrote *On the Banks of Plum Creek.*

Ever since readers learned that Walnut Grove was the town Laura described in *On the Banks of Plum Creek,* they have visited the community Laura simply referred to as "town." In 1953, Laura apologized to Everett Lantz of the *Walnut Grove Tribune* for omitting the name of the town. "I am sorry I did not mention the name of the town in my story," she said. "I should have, but at the time I had no idea I was writing history."

A museum and visitors' center has been established in Walnut Grove, in a former railroad depot.

An original quilt belonging to Laura is now on display in the Walnut Grove museum.

Charles and Caroline Ingalls were among the charter members of the Union Congregational Church of Walnut Grove when it was formed on August 24, 1874. The members decided to build a church immediately. As told in *On the Banks of Plum Creek,* Pa generously donated money to the church bell fund that he intended to spend on a pair of needed boots. The bell served the Congregational Church until the church disbanded in 1954. Since then, "Pa's church bell" has rung in the English Lutheran bell tower.

Garth Williams depicted the dedication and Christmas party held at the Congregational Church on December 20, 1874.

41

In her unpublished autobiography, *Pioneer Girl,* Laura vividly remembered the onset of the infamous grasshopper plague of 1875, which she said was "the worst ever known since the plagues of Egypt.

"We raised our faces and looked straight at the sun. It had been shining brightly, but now there was a light, fleecy cloud over it, so it did not hurt our eyes. Then we saw that the cloud was grasshoppers, their wings shining white, making a screen between us and the sun. They were dropping to the ground like hail in a hail storm, faster and faster."

Helen Sewell and Mildred Boyle depicted Laura and Mary Ingalls's visit to the Oleson store in Walnut Grove and an unpleasant encounter with the unfriendly Nellie, in the 1937 edition of *On the Banks of Plum Creek.* Laura first wrote of Nellie in one of her early columns for *The Missouri Ruralist.* She titled her story, "How Laura Got Even."

"I have lived among uncounted millions of grasshoppers. I have seen clouds of them darken the noonday sun. I saw their bodies choke the waters of Plum Creek, I saw them destroy every green thing on the face of the earth, so far as a child would know. There are unforgettable pictures of those grasshoppers in my mind that I have tried to draw plainly in *On the Banks of Plum Creek.*" (from *A Little House Sampler*)

One of Laura's girlhood treasures from Walnut Grove was the china jewel box she received at the Congregational Church Christmas party. In *On the Banks of Plum Creek* she wrote, "It was made of snow-white, gleaming china. On its top stood a wee, gold-coloured teapot and a gold-coloured tiny cup in a gold-coloured saucer." The china jewel box is on display at the Laura Ingalls Wilder Home and Museum in Mansfield, Missouri.

"The little white daisies with their hearts of gold grew thickly along the path where we walked to Sunday School. Father and sister and I used to walk the 2½ miles every Sunday morning. I can plainly see the path winding ahead, flecked with sunshine and shadow and the beautiful golden-hearted daisies scattered along the way."

CHAPTER 4

Little Hotel in the Village

Pa's dreams of successful wheat farming on the Minnesota prairie were destroyed by the grasshopper years. He was forced to walk hundreds of miles to eastern Minnesota, where he worked for wages as a harvest hand. In the fall of 1875 he came home again and moved Ma and the girls into a rented house in Walnut Grove. There they would have no fear of being stranded by blizzards in the house along Plum Creek.

Laura was away from home one day on an errand when her only brother was born. His name was Charles Frederick Ingalls, and the date was November 1, 1875.

When the 1876 crops were ruined once again, Pa said that he had had enough. "He just couldn't stay any longer in such a 'blasted country,'" Laura said. The Steadmans, friends from church, urged Pa and Ma to be their partners in the hotel business. Mr. Steadman had purchased the Masters Hotel in Burr Oak, Iowa, and Pa agreed to help operate the business.

Late in the summer, the Ingalls family traveled east in the covered wagon. "How I wished we were going west," Laura admitted. "Pa did not like to turn his back on the west either," she recalled. They stopped to visit Uncle Peter and Aunt Eliza Ingalls and the cousins along the Zumbro River near South Troy, Minnesota, when tragedy struck. Little Freddie, the only son and brother sickened; on August 27, 1876, he died. They left him in a lonely grave under a small white stone.

The drive from Uncle Peter's farm in southern Minnesota to Burr Oak, Iowa, was cold and dreary. The warm Masters Hotel was a welcoming sight to the Ingalls family, just as it was to the steady stream of pioneers traveling west. Burr Oak was at a crossroads; sometimes as many as 200 covered wagons stopped there overnight.

"Our hotel," Laura wrote, "the place Mr. Masters had sold to Mr. Steadman, was a very fine place. Our hotel was built on a side hill. A door from the main street opened into the bar-room, then across the hall was the parlor, also with a street door. At the back of the hall, stairs went to the bedrooms above and to the dining room below. It was a pretty place."

The Ingalls family lived in the shelter of the Masters Hotel several months; Pa and Ma disliked the constant flow of travelers and the sometimes rowdy barroom. Pa moved the family first to quiet rented rooms over a grocery store, then to a red brick house nearby.

Pa and Ma and their girls spent a year in Burr Oak before returning to Walnut Grove. Fifty-five years later, in 1932, Laura's daughter, Rose Wilder Lane, visited the town. She found the hotel and wandered through the village where her mother had lived as a ten-year-old. Still later, residents of Burr Oak and nearby Decorah grew increasingly interested in the fact that Laura Ingalls Wilder had once lived in the vicinity. They formed a group dedicated to the preservation of the old Masters Hotel. After much restoration, the hotel was opened as a historic site in 1976.

The old Masters Hotel as it appeared around the time Laura Ingalls lived there.

The restored Masters Hotel in Burr Oak.

In the lower-level dining room of the Masters Hotel, Laura and Mary helped serve meals to the many steady boarders and travelers who visited the pioneer inn.

Laura was ten years old during the year her family lived in Burr Oak. She often slipped away from the crowded Masters Hotel to walk in the Iowa countryside with her sisters and their friends from school. Many years later, she remembered that "I have thoughts of Burr Oak as a lovely place."

Taking the cows to their morning pastures and leading them home at day's end became Laura's chore. Of that experience Laura wrote: "It was a happy summer. I loved to go after the cows in the pasture by the creek where the rushes and blue flags grew and the grass was so fresh and smelled so sweet. . . ."

"Mary and I were going to school. It seemed to us a very big school, but as I remember there were only two rooms. The principal, whose name was Reid, was an elocutionist. I have always been grateful to him for the training I was given in reading."

The fourth and last daughter of the Ingalls family was born after Pa had moved the family away from the hotel to the red brick house. "One day," Laura wrote, "when I came back from an errand that had taken me a long time, I found a new little sister. We named her Grace. Her hair was golden like Mary's and her eyes were blue and bright like Pa's." Grace Pearl Ingalls was born on May 23, 1877. "I spent a great deal of time that summer caring for Baby Sister," Laura recalled.

Plain Protestant worship was always important to the Ingalls family. While they lived in Burr Oak, they attended this Congregational Church. Both the church and school building were razed years ago.

CHAPTER 5

Silver Lake and the Dakota Prairie

After a year in Burr Oak, the Ingalls family returned to Walnut Grove. They lived in town while Pa worked at a variety of jobs as a carpenter, store clerk, butcher, and miller. During the spring of 1879, there was sickness in the Ingalls house. Mary was stricken with what doctors called "brain fever." The ravages of the disease left the fourteen-year-old Mary blind.

It became Laura's duty to serve as Mary's eyes. Her mind was quick and she was able to describe the action and color and images of daily life to Mary. So Laura began seeing twice—once for herself, a second time for Mary.

By the Shores of Silver Lake recounted the Ingalls family's last move, west to Dakota Territory. During the summer of 1879, Pa was employed as timekeeper and paymaster for the Chicago and Northwestern Railroad being built west from Tracy, Minnesota, to Huron, Dakota. While Pa moved west with the railroad camps, Ma and the girls prepared to leave Walnut Grove. In September, the family was reunited at the railroad camp at Silver Lake, in eastern Dakota Territory.

Laura was twelve when she traveled west with her family for the final time. She was stout and capable. With keen interest she witnessed the building of the railroad and worked alongside Ma in the camp shanty. Faithfully, she interpreted the world for Mary. As Laura wrote in rhyme:

> If you've anything to do
> Do it with all your might
> Don't let trifles hinder you
> If you're sure it's right
> Work away
> Do it with all your might
> from an unpublished childhood
> collection of Laura's poetry

The frozen bed of Silver Lake is only rarely filled with water since its draining in 1923. In 1948, Laura wrote to an admirer that "the city drained Silver Lake and the Big Slough to get more plow land. As though the hundreds of acres of dry land were not enough!"

With the coming of the railroads and the white man's recreational hunting, the buffalo, which once grazed on the prairies, quickly disappeared from eastern Dakota Territory.

The Dakota Central Division of the Chicago and Northwestern Railroad brought the Ingalls family to the Silver Lake camp. In the spring of 1880, the town along the train tracks was formed. It was named De Smet, in honor of a Jesuit missionary priest from Belgium.

After arriving on Silver Lake, Laura noticed a tall, large house standing alone on the north bank of the water. It was the Surveyors' House, headquarters for the surveying crew working with the railroad building.

In the fall of 1879, when all the railroad work ended for the season, the head surveyor asked Pa if he would stay through the winter to guard the house, tools, and railroad property. The Ingallses agreed, making them the only family for miles around on the empty winter prairie.

In December of 1879, the family was settled in the Surveyors' House, which seemed very spacious to Laura. Coal and supplies were left along with books and papers to read that Pa had brought back from his last trip to civilization. Each evening, he placed a lighted lamp in the window, in case any lonely traveler was passing.

In the "spring rush" of 1880, Pa and Ma again operated a hotel, but this time in the Surveyors' House. It was the sole shelter for miles around, and the droves of homesteaders arriving to claim land paid 25¢ for a meal and 25¢ for a place to sleep.

In 1885, the Surveyors' House was moved from Silver Lake to its current locale in De Smet. In 1967, the Laura Ingalls Wilder Memorial Society restored the house as a literary landmark. It is the oldest building standing in De Smet.

Surveying equipment was stored in the lean-to of the house during the winter Laura and her family lived there.

One day, Mrs. Boast told them about whatnots. She said that everyone in Iowa was making whatnots, and she would show them how.

In the restored Surveyors' House, a replica of the whatnot stands in a corner.

The Surveyors' pantry was stocked with foodstuffs and supplies to last through the winter. It is arranged today just as Laura saw it for the first time when she arrived.

On display in the Surveyors' House is a chest of drawers made by Pa Ingalls. It was last used by Grace Ingalls Dow in her home in Manchester, South Dakota. Laura mentions finding her Christmas gift, a green-and-gilt copy of *Tennyson's Poems,* hidden in the bottom drawer in *Little Town on the Prairie.*

Ma's china shepherdess was a prized possession of the family. In her reply to a class who read her books, Laura mentioned that "Sister Carrie has the china shepherdess." Evidence indicates that the one shown here, found among Carrie's keepsakes in Keystone, South Dakota, is indeed the prototype for the cherished china figurine.

In the spring of 1880, the Ingalls family moved to their 160 acres of homestead land, a mile from De Smet. To the west of the land lay the Big Slough and to the north was Silver Lake. As described in *By the Shores of Silver Lake,* Pa built a shanty and planted cottonwood trees that served as a windbreak, one for each member of the family. From 1880 to 1887, the Ingallses lived on the homestead but spent some of the winters in De Smet. Pa sold the land in 1892.

"They're cottonwoods," Pa said. "They all grew from seeds of the Lone Tree that we saw across the prairie when we were coming out from Brookings. It's a giant of a tree when you get close to it. It's seeded all along to the edge of Lake Henry. I dug enough of these seedlings to make a windbreak clear around the shanty. You're going to have your trees growing, Caroline, quick as I can get them set in the ground."

In 1957, the Laura Ingalls Wilder Memorial Society was founded in De Smet to establish a monument to the author of the Little House books. The site selected was a corner of the original Ingalls homestead. Since then, thousands of visiting readers have worn a path up the low hill to the prairie rock memorial.

Aubrey Sherwood of the *De Smet News* wrote the text of the marker explaining the history of the Ingalls family and their land. The plaque was affixed to a boulder found at nearby Spirit Lake and dedicated in 1958.

Helen Sewell and Mildred Boyle, first illustrators of the Little House books, depicted a claim shanty in the first edition of *By the Shores of Silver Lake,* published in 1939.

The Ingalls homestead was located in the Lake Henry neighborhood and their mail was addressed to a small post-office station called Lake Henry.

In the fall of 1947, the artist Garth Williams visited Laura and Almanzo Wilder in Mansfield, Missouri, to prepare the creation of newly designed and illustrated editions of the Little House books. From Laura, the artist obtained directions to her writing locales.

Mr. Williams spent two days in De Smet. Aubrey Sherwood, the local newspaper publisher, directed the illustrator to historic sites and shared information with him. Later, Garth Williams wrote to Laura: "De Smet . . . was exciting. Naturally all your books are well known. Mr. Sherwood very kindly spent a long time personally conducting me around. He showed me where your father's first claim shanty was. Others in town were able to point out the few original stores remaining and describe the difference today.

"I drove South to the shores of Lake Henry and on beyond to where your first school must have been. I almost saw Almanzo driving out to fetch you home across the endless snow.

"For a long time I peered into the windows of the house just south of the big slough; and I have never seen or known such an enormous sky. Although the country must look settled to you today, I completely felt the minuteness of people & carts & houses—out in a prairie."

Garth Williams posed at the house which stood on the Ingalls homestead land on his 1947 visit *(above)* and the Big Slough, with the Ingalls homestead on the horizon, looking south, as photographed by Garth Williams *(right).*

CHAPTER 6

The Long, Hard Winter

The Long Winter, Laura Ingalls Wilder's sixth book, was published in 1940. It recounted the infamous "Hard Winter" of 1880–81, which paralyzed wide sections of the Midwest with frigid force. Storms often caught the prairie pioneers unprepared and some newcomers to the land froze to death or nearly starved on isolated homestead claims. For six months, unrelenting winter weather tested the survival skills of the homesteaders.

The first blizzard of the season struck on October 15, 1880. The Ingalls family shivered and huddled together in the flimsy shelter of their claim shanty near De Smet. When the storm subsided and Pa Ingalls visited De Smet, he encountered an old Indian who warned of "heap big snow" and a long winter. Pa believed the Indian omens. He decided to move his family from the isolated homestead claim a mile from town to his solidly built business building at the corner of Main and Second streets.

After the Ingalls family settled into town life, Laura and Carrie attended De Smet's first school and were taught by Miss Florence Garland. But blizzards struck with increasing frequency. The railroads from the East which brought fuel and food supplies were stalled on the tracks in mounds of snow. As soon as snowplows and men with shovels could clear the tracks, another blizzard would sweep in to pile the cuts with icy snow. Christmas passed without the arrival of supply trains—or the Christmas barrel of surprises the Ingalls family had counted on.

The stores in De Smet grew empty of goods. School was canceled until coal arrived. At the Ingalls home, the kerosene can was empty, coal was running low, and food was scarce. In January of 1881, the news was telegraphed to De Smet that the Chicago and Northwestern Railroad Company was giving up; they would not attempt to clear the snowbanks away any longer. There would be no trains running until spring. Spring was four months away.

The Ingalls family spent the winter working desperately to keep warm and fed. When all their foodstuffs were eaten, Ma baked a daily loaf of bread from wheat ground into flour with a coffee mill. The monotonous sound of the grinding mill sounded all day in the narrow kitchen where Pa and Ma and their girls tried to keep warm around the stove. In the cold lean-to, Pa and Laura busily twisted long strands of hay into sticks. The tightly stranded hay burned faster than kindling and made a feeble fire.

> Then what is the use of repining
> For where there's a will there's a way
> And tomorrow the sun may be shining
> Although it is cloudy today.
>
> from *The Long Winter*

Pa often sang "Where There's a Will There's a Way" through the dark, lonely, blizzard-bound months. Working together, the Ingalls family and the entire pioneer community of De Smet survived the terrible winter.

"The colder the weather will be, the thicker the muskrats build the walls of their houses," Pa told Laura. "I never saw a heavier-built muskrats' house than that one." Muskrats still follow their natural instinct for protection against the hard winters on the prairies of South Dakota. These muskrat houses are near the edge of Lake Henry, south of De Smet.

The Ingalls building originally stood on Main and Second streets in De Smet. There the Ingalls family weathered the winter. At the time this photograph was

taken in 1912, the building had been moved to the rear of the lot, to make way for a brick bank structure. Later yet, the Ingalls building served as a real estate office and was finally torn down and the lumber used to construct another house in De Smet.

Laura recalled that "A handful of hay was twisted into a rope, then doubled over and allowed to twist back on itself and the two ends came together in a knot, making what we called 'a stick of hay.' " In 1916 she wrote: "It was a busy job to keep a supply of these 'sticks' ahead of a hungry stove. But everyone took his turn good naturedly. There is something in living close to the great elemental forces of nature that causes people to rise above small annoyances and discomforts."

The Hard Winter
Chapter One
Making Hay.

The whirr of the mowing machine sounded cheerfully from the old buffalo wallow south of the claim shanty. Blue stem grass stood thick and tall there and Pa was cutting it for hay.

Laura brought a pailful of water from the well at the edge of the Big Slough. She rinsed the stone water jug to cool it, then filled it full of the fresh water, corked it tightly and started with it for the hay field. The sunshine was bright and hot and Pa would be thirsty, for it was only three oclock of a hot afternoon. There would be hours yet of mowing before Pa would stop work for night.

As Laura carried the jug of water to the field, she watched the clouds of white butterflies hovering over the path and a dragon fly with lovely, gauzy wings chasing a gnat. Laura knew they were dragon-flies because Ma said so, but Pa called them Devil's darning needles and Laura

Pleasures were simple and rare for the Ingalls family during the "Hard Winter." The girls studied their school books in the dim light and memorized poetry and prose to recite back to Ma. When Pa's stiff and frostbitten fingers could no longer play the fiddle, they all sang bravely together to drown out the shrieking blizzard winds. A bundle of *The Youth's Companion* had arrived in the last mail delivery which reached De Smet; through the long winter months, the stories were doled out sparingly and read aloud so that the whole family could enjoy them.

Laura Ingalls Wilder wrote all of her Little House books in pencil on lined nickel school tablets. Her first working title for *The Long Winter* had been *The Hard Winter*. Her editors at Harper and Brothers requested a title change because they objected to presenting anything difficult or hard to young readers. In 1949, Laura presented her original manuscript for *The Long Winter* to the Detroit Public Library, where it is now preserved in the Rare Book and Gift Room.

A stranded freight train on the prairie during the "Hard Winter" of 1880–81.

Not long after they had settled on the Dakota prairies, the Ingalls family posed for a traveling tintype artist. Carrie stands at left, Mary is seated in the center, and Laura is at right.

Pa and Ma, Charles and Caroline Ingalls, "possessed the pioneering spirit to a marked degree," said Laura.

Who can describe a Winter, of the North, upon the plains?
How tell the fury of the winds, when the Storm King reigns?
How sing the song of a whirling world of snow?
Or catch the rhythmic measure that the storm winds blow?

Laura Ingalls Wilder

During the "Hard Winter" food became dangerously depleted in De Smet. Even the carefully saved stocks of seed wheat were ground up and baked into bread. In February, young Almanzo Wilder and his chum Cap Garland made a dangerous trip across the frozen prairie in search of a supply of wheat and bought sixty bushels from a homesteader living on an isolated claim. Their bravery saved the town of De Smet from starvation.

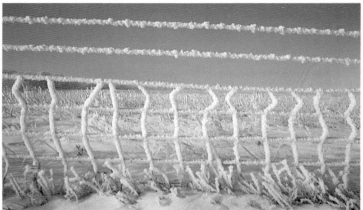

During the monotonous, dreary days when the blizzard winds blew and made the crowded kitchen of the Ingalls house gloomy and dusky, Laura cheered her sisters and helped Pa and Ma. In her school tablet she wrote these lines of poetry:

> We remember not the summer
> For it was long ago
> We remember not the summer
> In this whirling blinding snow
> I will leave this frozen region
> I will travel farther south
> If you say one word against it
> I will hit you in the mouth

CHAPTER 7

De Smet: Laura's Little Town on the Prairie

Laura Ingalls Wilder's *Little Town on the Prairie* tells of the settlement and development of De Smet, the seat of Kingsbury County. From the earliest beginnings of the town, Pa Ingalls was a leader. He served as the town clerk, justice of the peace, deputy sheriff, street commissioner, and was active in the founding of the Congregational Church.

During the winters, the Ingalls family moved to the town of De Smet, and though Laura always preferred life in the country, she considered town to be an interesting interlude. She and Carrie attended the first school, and there were birthday parties, church socials, literary societies, and entertainments to enjoy.

Mary was not a part of the family life in De Smet, for during the fall of 1881, Pa and Ma took her to Vinton, Iowa, to enroll in the Iowa College for the Blind. There she reveled in her studies and received expert training for life as a sightless person.

While the town of De Smet thrived, so did Pa's homestead. On the claim, crops grew lustily. Pa enlarged the shanty until it could rightfully be called a little house. And during the summers, while she studied to become a teacher, Laura found time to help Pa with the farm work. She was proud to take part in creating a farm out of the fierce, tough prairie land.

Laura's De Smet in 1883 was sketched by a traveling artist from Wisconsin. The First Congregational Church, which Pa helped build, is marked "A." The schoolhouse is across from the church. The railroad depot is where Laura attended her first party. Pa's business building, at the corner of Main and Second streets, is just behind the K.

The earliest known photograph of Calumet Avenue (Main Street) in De Smet was taken in 1883.

The original depot was destroyed by fire on Easter Sunday, 1905, and was replaced by this building, now the headquarters of the De Smet City Museum.

Main Street of *Little Town on the Prairie.*

The gracious Kingsbury County Court House was built in 1898. The Ingalls family knew this landmark well.

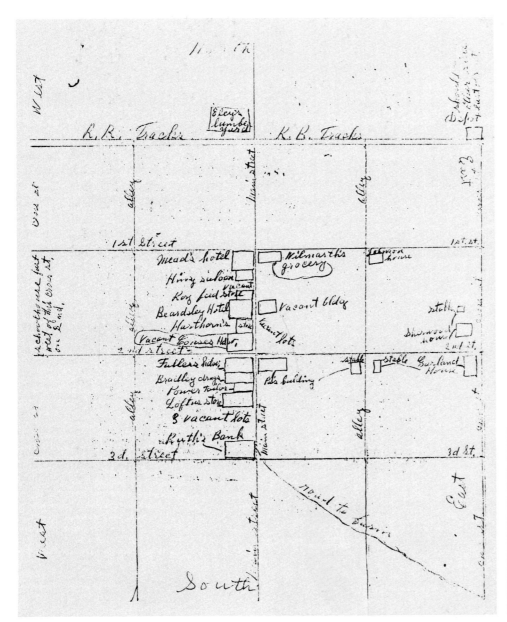

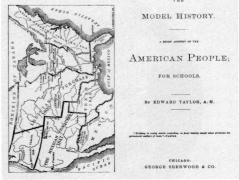

In writing *The Long Winter* and *Little Town on the Prairie,* Laura included maps of the town of De Smet in her penciled drafts to help her recall with accuracy the houses and businesses along Main Street.

For the school exhibition described in *Little Town on the Prairie,* Laura recited over half of United States history before the community of De Smet. In 1949, she presented her history book and other memorabilia to the Detroit Public Library.

De Smet's first school was attended by Laura and Carrie Ingalls *(above).* It was located across from the Congregational Church on Second Street. As the town grew, the school became too small and in 1885 it was sold and converted to a residence. The building now stands on Third Street. In the process of redecorating the interior, owners found the original blackboards under layers of wallpaper! Among Laura's pleasures while growing up in De Smet was the exchange of name cards with friends from school *(left).*

The interior of a general store in De Smet shows the variety of merchandise available to the settlers of the *Little Town on the Prairie.*

Although Laura far preferred the quiet, busy life on the homestead claim with Ma and her sisters, she took her first job in town sewing with the dressmaker, Mrs. White. *Little Town on the Prairie* describes her early morning walks into town with Pa. Pa was hired to help build the Congregational Church building, and Laura added nine dollars to Mary's college fund by sewing shirts and making button holes.

Renowned artist, teacher, and illustrator Harvey Dunn (1884–1952) was born and reared on the prairie near Manchester, South Dakota, seven miles from De Smet. He knew the Ingalls family well, for his uncle Nate Dow married Laura's sister Grace. Although throughout Dunn's long illustrating career he painted a variety of subjects, he admitted that "I find that I prefer painting pictures of early South Dakota life to any other kind, which would seem to point to the fact that my search of other horizons has led me around to my first."

Dunn's canvas entitled *Something for Supper* depicts a scene Pa Ingalls loved: a day of hunting on the prairie. This painting was among a large collection exhibited by Harvey Dunn in De Smet in 1950 and given to the people of South Dakota for exhibition at South Dakota State University, Brookings.

Prints of Dunn's *The Prairie Is My Garden,* as well as *Something for Supper,* were framed by Laura and hung on the walls of her Rocky Ridge farmhouse. Said Laura: "Harvey Dunn has done a great thing in his paintings and it does seem as though they and my stories should be connected in some way. I should be proud to have our names connected because of our work."

Oh! It's long bright days,
Of sunshine on the prairies,
In the summer . . .

Oh prairies green
Or prairies brown,
Our love for you ne'er wearies!

Because of sunshine
And moonshine
And starshine
And the prairies,
The days and nights are perfect,
On the prairies,
In the summer . . .

Free verse by Laura Ingalls Wilder

69

AUTUMN

Ever I see them, with my memory's vision,
As first my eyes beheld them, years agone,
Clad all in brown, with russet shades and
    golden,
Stretching away into the far unknown.

Never a break to mar their sweep of
    grandeur,
From North to South, from East to West,
    the same,
Save that the East was full of purple
    shadows,
The West, with setting sun, was all aflame.

Never a sign of human habitation,
To show that man's dominion was begun,
The only marks, the footpaths of the Bison,
Made by the herds, before their day was
    done.

The sky downturned, a brazen bowl above
    me;
And clanging with the calls of wild gray
    geese,
Winging their way into the distant
    South-land,
To 'scape the coming storms and rest in
    peace.

Ever the winds went whispering o'er the
    prairie,
Ever the grasses whispered back again;
And then the sun dipped down below the
    sky-line;
And stars lit just the outlines of the plain.

> Excerpt from a longer poem
> of Laura's, "From the Dakota Prairie"

The Ingalls homestead land as photographed by illustrator Garth Williams in November 1947. A corner of the original homestead, a mile south of De Smet, is now the Ingalls Homestead Memorial Site.

CHAPTER 8

Laura, Almanzo, and Rose

A replica of the first school at which Laura taught was constructed in De Smet. In *These Happy Golden Years,* Laura referred to the school and the family she lived with as "Brewster." In reality she taught at the Bouchie School, but because of the Bouchie family's unpleasant characters and a later scandal surrounding them, Laura changed the name in her book.

The last of Laura Ingalls Wilder's eight-volume Little House series was *These Happy Golden Years,* published in 1943. The story describes Laura's first experiences as a country school-teacher in an isolated abandoned claim shanty called The Brewster School. Laura was just fifteen when she started teaching the two-month term of school in the winter of 1883, and she was homesick while living twelve miles from home. But she was determined to earn the $40 promised her, to help with Mary's expenses at the Iowa College for the Blind.

Laura's three teaching jobs at the Brewster School, the Perry School, and the Wilkins School were enlivened by the Friday afternoon arrivals of Almanzo Wilder, who offered to drive her home. Almanzo, a prosperous homesteader ten years older than Laura, drove the finest team of matched Morgan horses in Kingsbury County. When winter snow covered the prairie, he hitched his team to a swift cutter. In the springtime, the horses pulled a flashy buggy.

Laura was often bashful and shy with Almanzo. Once she bluntly told him she rode with him only to get home for the weekends. But Almanzo continued to court. In the summer, they drove to Spirit Lake, north of De Smet, and to the Twin Lakes, Henry and Thompson.

Laura was seventeen when Almanzo asked her to marry him. She agreed, but made him promise that their wedding ceremony would not ask that she obey him.

Almanzo James Wilder at the time of *These Happy Golden Years.* Laura called him Manly.

Laura Elizabeth Ingalls in 1884, at the age of seventeen. Almanzo called her Bessie.

"One Sunday that summer a team and buggy came dashing around the corner of the livery barn in town, and out along the road across the Big Slough. I could see it plainly from the dooryard where I happened to be. The buggy was new, for the sunshine flashed and sparkled from wheels and top. The horses were beautiful, trotting so swiftly and evenly. The team turned in toward our house and I wondered who could be coming. Then I saw it was Manly. . . . "(from *Pioneer Girl*)

"Your description of the old prairie road made me homesick," Laura confided to Aubrey Sherwood, publisher and editor of the *De Smet News.*

After their marriage on August 25, 1885, Almanzo and Laura Wilder started their life together as farmers. Their first home was in the "little gray house in the west" on Almanzo's tree claim a mile north of De Smet. Their experiences in the first years of their married life are recounted in *The First Four Years.* (This book was published in 1971, fourteen years after Laura's death, from her original penciled manuscripts.)

The Wilders were plagued with a series of disasters during those seasons of Dakota homesteading. There were crop failures and harsh weather, heavy debts and drought. Almanzo and Laura nearly died from diphtheria; Almanzo's health was permanently weakened by a stroke, which was probably a case of polio.

On December 5, 1886, Rose, the Wilders' only daughter, was born. She was named for the flowers that covered the summer prairies. A son was born and lived only briefly in August of 1889; two weeks later, the Wilders' house burned.

"Heartbreaking" was the way Laura summed up her first years with Almanzo on their prairie farm. "No one," she stated, "who has not homesteaded, can understand the fascination and the terror of it."

On the low hill stood the claim shanty, the birthplace of Rose Wilder. The historical marker, along South Dakota Highway 25, recounts the experiences of the Wilders on this land.

Some of Almanzo's plantings still survive on the Wilder tree claim. A shallow indentation on the prairie remains where the "little gray house" once stood before the 1889 fire. Revisiting the site with Almanzo in 1931, Laura noted: "The tree claim is still grass . . . there are no buildings [on it] and only a few trees left."

Laura and Almanzo posed for the De Smet photographer the winter following their wedding.

The *De Smet News and Leader* noted the marriage of Laura Ingalls and Almanzo Wilder.

Laura called June on the prairie "The Month of Roses." "You are named for them, my dear," she told Rose.

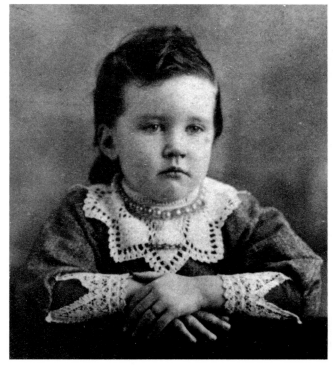

This picture of Rose was taken when the Wilders were visiting Almanzo's parents in Spring Valley, Minnesota.

CHAPTER 9

The House on Third Street

"Pa and Ma and the girls lived for some years in the little house on the homestead," Laura wrote, "but later Pa built a house in the residential part of town and they lived there to be nearer church and neighbors." That last move of the Ingalls family to a pleasant frame house along Third Street in De Smet occurred at Christmastime, 1887. Never again did Pa and Ma stir from their final home together. Pa died there in 1902; Ma in 1924. The house Pa built, with its tall windows, cleverly built closets and cupboards, wallpapered rooms, and twisting stairways was home to members of the family for forty years. From this house Pa went to work each morning at his carpentry jobs,

while Ma was busy with the housework. Mary returned here to live happily after she finished college. Carrie lived at home for years, while she worked as a newspaper employee at the *De Smet News.* Grace grew up in the De Smet house, graduated from high school, and was married in the parlor one evening in 1901.

Although Laura never lived in her parents' last house, she and Almanzo and Rose thought of it as home. "You'll never see a more cheerful home," Rose remarked of the Ingalls house in De Smet.

In 1973, the Laura Ingalls Wilder Memorial Society of De Smet restored the Ingalls home for visitor touring.

Behind the house was a big garden and the well and pump.

In the kitchen, Pa constructed these cupboards for Ma's use. She was proud of her husband's workmanship, and Mary easily memorized the contents of the cupboards, to help Ma with the housework.

In the parlor stood Mary's organ, and the family often gathered around to sing while she played hymns.

In 1915, a wall telephone was installed in the Ingalls dining room for the convenience of Ma and Mary, then living in the house alone.

In the parlor, Pa and Ma's portraits look down from the walls of their longtime home.

The Ingalls home has been restored painstakingly to the way it appeared in the 1890s and early 1900s.

Many of the original possessions of the Ingalls family are exhibited in their restored De Smet home. A lap writing desk, clothes, beadwork made by Mary, and autograph books are on display.

"Pa and Ma were great readers and I read a lot at home with them," Laura wrote. Many of the Ingalls family's books are still found in their home.

The bedroom off the parlor was used by Pa and Ma.

A close-up of one of Mary's and Laura's and Carrie's little glass boxes. "Each box had frosted flowers on its side and colored flowers on the lid."

Mary's bedroom was on the first floor of the Ingalls home.

The narrow twisting stairway led to three upstairs bedrooms in the Ingalls home. For many years, Pa and Ma rented extra rooms to boarders in their home, adding to Pa's wages as a carpenter.

Following Rose Wilder Lane's death in 1968, many of her furnishings and possessions from her longtime home in Danbury, Connecticut, were sent to De Smet for exhibit. Rooms from Rose's home were simulated in the upstairs of the Ingalls home. At Rose's large, personally designed desk, she wrote *On the Way Home, Woman's Day Book of American Needlework,* and worked on the revision of *The Discovery of Freedom.*

One of Rose's favorite Underwood typewriters was bequeathed to her friend, journalist and author Norma Lee Browning, who donated it to the Rose Wilder Lane exhibit.

Restored Ingalls bedroom looks as it did when Laura, Almanzo, and Rose Wilder visited this home.

The first editions of the Little House books were illustrated by Helen Sewell and Mildred Boyle. This exhibit features the early editions and the later uniform set, illustrated by Garth Williams.

Since the Surveyors' House in De Smet was opened for tours in 1968, thousands of Laura's readers have visited her childhood homesites in the prairie town of which she wrote. Next to the Surveyors' House is the headquarters of the Laura Ingalls Wilder Memorial Society. Situated in a typical Victorian home of the era, the society headquarters offers information, orientation, and exhibits pertaining to the history of Laura's De Smet years.

Original chinaware used by the Ingalls family is displayed in De Smet.

One volume of the original set of eight that comprised The Holy Bible, printed in embossed print and used by Mary Ingalls, is proudly exhibited in De Smet.

CHAPTER 10

Caroline L. Ingalls

Charles P. Ingalls

From the Family Album

The Ingalls family posed for their only group picture in De Smet, probably just before Laura left for Mansfield, Missouri, in 1894. At left is Ma; next to her is Carrie who was employed at the *De Smet News.* Laura is behind Pa, wearing her black wedding dress; Pa is wearing his prized Masonic emblem on his vest. Grace, a high school student, stands next to Mary.

An old postcard shows the shady residential Third Street that was journey's end for the Ingalls family. The Ingalls yard is plainly visible under the bower of trees; the gable end of their house and the east window are to the left of the porch of the Perry house next door. "Do you think the trees have grown since you were here?" Ma asked Laura about this scene.

While a student at the Iowa College for the Blind at Vinton, Mary posed at the Starr Gallery for a photograph. Laura wrote: "Mary graduated from the Iowa College for the Blind in 1889. Her part in an entertainment given by her literary society was an essay entitled 'Memory.'"

Mary never regained her eyesight, nor did she marry. "After graduation," Laura explained, "Mary lived happily at home with her music, and her raised print and Braille books. She knitted and sewed and took part in the housework."

Mary wrote poetry, corresponded with blind friends in Braille, and wrote letters to seeing friends with the help of her grooved slate. This 1904 letter was sent to Minnie Green, who, with her lawyer-husband, had rented rooms in the Ingalls house when they first came to town in 1902.

Carrie Ingalls, photographed in De Smet during the 1890s.

Carrie's career as a pioneer newspaperwoman started in De Smet but extended to many papers in western South Dakota.

Carrie married Black Hills mine owner David Swanzey in 1912. They lived happily in the mining town of Keystone, at the foot of Mount Rushmore. Dave Swanzey is credited with naming the mountain.

Carrie's marriage brought her two stepchildren to raise. This 1912 photo shows Carrie at the right, her stepson Harold next to her, and stepdaughter Mary, third from the left.

Carrie's Keystone, South Dakota, home was destroyed by fire in 1977, but a marker notes her long connection with the Black Hills town.

Carrie, standing at left, posed with a group of De Smet friends in the 1890s.

Grace Ingalls graduated from the De Smet High School and attended the small Congregational Redfield College, where she studied to be a teacher. She taught several terms of school in the Manchester area, seven miles from De Smet. There she met farmer Nate Dow. They were married at the Ingalls home on October 16, 1901.

Nate and Grace Dow at home in March 1908. Grace sent this postcard picture to her niece Rose Wilder, signing it "Aunty Fat."

The Dow farmstead was located a mile from the village of Manchester, near the Redstone Creek. Grace lived there for many years as a farm wife. Ma, Mary, Carrie, and Laura all visited here.

Grace Ingalls.

One day when Grace was very young, she was reading in the Dakota claim shanty and looked up at Ma to ask, "What is a tree?" Her little-girl images were of great sweeps of treeless Dakota land; she knew nothing of the Wisconsin woods. Laura provided her sister with a graphic answer: On tin, she painted this scene, which shows the rushing water, the hills, and foliage all foreign to a prairie child.

Almanzo and Laura Wilder as they looked in the early 1890s. Laura is wearing her black wedding dress. Of their marriage Laura said: "We'll always be farmers, for what is bred in the bone will come out in the flesh."

To help recover Almanzo's weakened health, the Wilders decided to leave the drought-stricken South Dakota prairies. In 1890, Laura, Almanzo, and Rose journeyed to Spring Valley, Minnesota, where they spent a year with Almanzo's parents on their fertile farm. From there they traveled to the Florida panhandle and lived in "The Piney Woods" near the village of Westville. "I was something of a curiosity, being the only 'Yankee girl' the inhabitants had ever seen," Laura commented. Before returning to live in De Smet during the summer of 1892, the Wilders posed for this photo with the Florida landscape in the background.

An oval glass bread plate survived the fire that burned the "Little Gray Home in the West" described in *The First Four Years*. For daily bread Laura and Almanzo worked steadily after their return to De Smet. Laura sewed at the dressmaker's and Almanzo worked at day labor. Their goal was to save enough to leave the prairie and establish a new farm in the Ozark hills of Missouri.

Laura and Almanzo longed for a new home in a climate less harsh than the South Dakota plains. Laura's painting on tin perhaps portrays what she considered "our ideal home."

Laura and Almanzo both shared a love for fine horses. Laura copied this famous Currier & Ives print entitled *The Storm.*

"As the sun rises," Laura wrote, "you feel the turning of the earth. You feel the whole globe under your feet, moving into the sunlight." Laura Ingalls Wilder left the prairie sunrises in 1894, to see instead the sunrises over the Ozark hills of Missouri.

CHAPTER 11

Little House in the Ozarks

Laura's lap writing desk, which traveled in the covered wagon from De Smet to Mansfield, contained a carefully hidden $100 bill to buy a new farm in the Ozarks.

In July 1894, Almanzo, Laura, and Rose Wilder left De Smet and traveled by covered wagon to a new home and a new life in Mansfield, Missouri. Their new farmland was in the heart of the Ozark Mountain country. The Wilders purchased a rough, hilly, stony, and wooded forty acres of land, which Laura promptly named Rocky Ridge Farm. Her traveling days as a pioneer were over.

Almanzo and Laura approached farming as a team, and they made their Ozark land thrive. Laura became an expert dairymaid, poultry breeder, and a renowned homemaker. At the age of forty-four, in 1911, she launched her literary career and a long association writing for the *Missouri Ruralist.* Her essays, poetry, and columns celebrated country living and farm life, and brought "Mrs. A. J. Wilder" regional fame as an authority on rural subjects.

When the farming years were over, Laura reaped the last harvest of her long life: the writing of the Little House books. All of her writing was done in the secluded country setting of the Wilders' beloved Rocky Ridge Farm.

Mansfield, Missouri.

"There is no other country in the world like the Ozarks," Laura wrote. "But the Ozarks are not really mountains, they are valleys. So the skyline is always level and blue like the sea, and nearly always there is a lovely blue haze all over the hillsides cut so deeply in this old, old land."

In the quiet hollows and shady lanes of Rocky Ridge Farm, Laura found inspiration for essays and poetry which were published for the readers of the *Missouri Ruralist.* The fall of the year was her favorite time . . .

> Sweet is the Autumn
> when the leaves turn red
> And the squirrels leap and chatter,
> While the ripe nuts fall
> from the leaves overhead
> And drop on the ground
> with a patter.

For her column in the *Missouri Ruralist,* Laura described autumn on Rocky Ridge: "There is a purple haze over the hill tops and a hint of sadness in the sunshine because of summer's departure. . . . Here and there the leaves are beginning to change color and a little, vagrant, autumn breeze goes wandering over the hills and down the valleys, whispering to 'follow, follow' until it is almost impossible to resist."

The Wilder farm grew to 200 acres and the house on the wooded knoll was built from materials from the land. The house took fifteen years to complete; Almanzo and Laura added rooms when money, time, and materials were available. The *Mansfield Mirror* noted the last phase of construction of the Wilder home on September 25, 1913: "A. J. Wilder is building a fine 12-room residence on his farm. . . . Mr. Wilder is one of our most progressive farmers."

"Our ideal home is one built by a man and woman together," Laura believed. She and Almanzo spent the remainder of their long lives here. After Laura's death, the house was preserved by the Laura Ingalls Wilder Home Association and opened to Little House readers.

A museum was constructed next to the Wilder house to hold the memorabilia and relics of Almanzo, Laura, and Rose. Rose Wilder Lane's generosity made possible the preservation project of the family home.

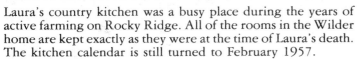

Laura's country kitchen was a busy place during the years of active farming on Rocky Ridge. All of the rooms in the Wilder home are kept exactly as they were at the time of Laura's death. The kitchen calendar is still turned to February 1957.

In her later years, Laura usually sat in her favorite rocking chair in the dining room. The big dining table was often heaped with piles of fan mail from Little House readers.

The screened porch off the dining room was a comfortable place during the hot Ozark summers. Laura sometimes served meals on the porch, which opened to the shady yard and the long, sloping hill leading to Highway 60.

The big parlor was the tenth and last room added to the Rocky Ridge farmhouse in 1913. It was the scene of many social gatherings and parties throughout the Wilders' busy years of farming. Laura loved to dance and occasionally the music of fiddlers and the sounds of square dancing filled the room. At Christmastime, 1920, Laura wrote Ma and her sisters: "After dinner we sat by the fire in the fireplace and read and looked at our Christmas cards and letters. Then later we popped corn over the fire and ate apples and walnuts. . . ."

The rustic stairway leads to an upstairs guest bedroom and Rose Wilder Lane's writing studio, where she wrote *Let the Hurricane Roar* and countless articles, short stories, and books.

Almanzo made some of the furniture in the house, including this cypress knee table. The cypress stump was brought from a Florida swamp by Almanzo.

95

In her writing den, just off the bedroom, Laura did much of the work of writing the Little House books, as well as many thousands of letters.

In one corner niche of the big living room sat an old pump organ dating from the 1890s. The Victrola next to the organ played the Wilders' collection of classical, popular, and folk music recordings. The Wilders called this area of the house the music room.

The Wilders' bedroom featured twin beds, matching handmade chairs for Laura and Almanzo, and Laura's dressing tables. The white door leads to the bathroom.

Across from the music room was the library, an area of five-foot-high shelves for Laura's many books. Eventually the library included many curios and souvenirs from Rose's international travels, and awards and honors given to Laura in recognition of her career as an author.

Laura's books range from the works of classic authors to mysteries and western tales. Some of her most treasured keepsakes were books belonging to Ma, dating from the 1850s and 1860s.

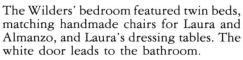

The clock that Almanzo gave to Laura for their first Christmas together in De Smet. This clock traveled with the Wilders to Missouri in 1894. Every night until he died, Almanzo wound the striking clock.

Rocky Ridge Farm was one mile east of the town square of Mansfield, Missouri, "The Gem City of the Ozarks." In 1898, the Wilders moved to town so that Rose could be nearer to school and Almanzo could pursue his draying and delivery business. Laura cooked meals for the officials of the Bluebird Railroad and boarded the local banker during the early 1900s. The Wilders were impor- tant in the social life of the little town: They were active in the Methodist Church, the Masonic Order, the Eastern Star, and the Red Cross. Laura helped found the educa- tional club called Justamere Club. She was also a charter member of The Athenians, a group dedicated to the establishment of a Wright County library. The club was organized in 1916.

Though they lived in town for many years, the Wilders continued to improve and expand Rocky Ridge Farm. Many acres of the land were cleared of timber, and rail fences enclosed the Wilder orchards, fields, and pastures. Laura and Almanzo worked on the farm whenever they could spare the time.

Of the rustic, quiet home on Rocky Ridge Farm, Laura wrote: "On one low hill that in springtime is covered with a blue carpet of wild violets, there is a white farmhouse; a U.S. highway curves at the foot of the hill. Behind the house is a gulch where a little spring wanders, and behind the gulch rises a steep, high hill where tall oaks grow, and dogwoods and redbuds that bloom in the spring. Almanzo and I live in this white farmhouse."

"The farm is grand, really," Rose Wilder Lane explained to her cosmopolitan writing friends. "Quite cool and remote and covered with big trees. . . ."

"The oak frame of the house, oak paneling, solid oak beams and stairs in the living room are from our own timber, hand finished," Laura said proudly. "An enormous fireplace is made of three rocks dug from our own ground. I had my heart set on having a fireplace made of rock off the farm, but The Man of the Place had become tired of hauling rocks and to my consternation returned from town one day with a load of fire-bricks to use instead. I objected strenuously; I argued; I begged; I declared that if it was too much work to build the fireplace as it should be then we would have none. At last when everything else failed, I wept. . . . And to my surprise it worked." This picture shows the fireplace in the parlor during the 1930s.

Laura kept most of the windows in the house without heavy drapes. "I don't want curtains over my pictures," she declared. Outside were "landscapes of forest and meadow and hills curving against the sky."

Laura said: "The open stairs at the south end of the room have a landing four steps up and turn here at right angles. On the landing is a door leading to my office. All the woodwork is solid oak finished in the natural color."

All through the Rocky Ridge farmhouse, Almanzo's carpentry and cabinetry skills were evident. "The Man of the Place is a good jack-knife carpenter," Laura said. She was proud of all the convenient and loving features Almanzo built into her dream house. The dining room cupboards were among the carefully thought out and wrought examples of Laura and Almanzo's teamwork.

"I gave the whole cabinet, inside and out," Laura wrote in 1925, "two coats of white paint and then enameled it. . . . I had a sideboard, china closet and linen closet combined."

Though she worked busily with her housekeeping, Laura was always Almanzo's most willing partner in the farm work. She helped him during haying season, just as she had worked with Pa when she was young. "The hay is in and the sun still shining," Laura wrote to Rose when she sent this picture of the barn on Rocky Ridge to her daughter.

One of Laura's early journalistic triumphs was publishing two articles in the important weekly magazine *The Country Gentleman,* in 1925. "My Ozark Kitchen" and "The Farm Dining Room" each described the evolution of those rooms in the Wilder home.

These photographs were taken for use as magazine illustrations and show the kitchen as Laura was using it in 1925. Her countertops were low to accommodate her five-foot stature; the windows looked out on the trees and hills she loved. The broom closet at left was later transformed into space for a refrigerator.

Almanzo piped spring water through the wood stove and into the sink so that hot water would flow through the tap. The pass-through opened into the dining room.

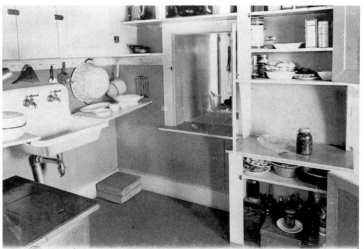

When the farmhouse was wired for electricity, Laura happily stowed away her oil lamps in the cupboard above the sink. It had been a smelly daily job to clean and fill and trim the wicks for each lamp.

"We worked hard, but it was interesting and didn't hurt us any," Laura said of the years she and Almanzo spent in building up their 200-acre Rocky Ridge Farm. Almanzo is shown with horses Buck and Billy, and Nero, the family dog.

Almanzo, driving the hay cart.

The well house and the woodpile also show the structure of the original two-room farmhouse constructed by Almanzo on Rocky Ridge Farm.

When Laura started writing for the *Missouri Ruralist* in 1911, she often submitted articles about her friends, her family, her home, and the farm at Rocky Ridge. One of her articles dealt with "My Ozark Apple Orchard." It was published in 1912, with this picture of Almanzo on the cover of the issue. The twelve-year-old tree bore seven barrels of apples during one picking. The Wilder orchard successfully shipped carloads of fruit to big city markets in St. Louis and Memphis.

This is the first barn on Rocky Ridge Farm. The farm raised cows, hogs, chickens, turkeys, sheep, and horses in addition to fruit and field crops.

Almanzo J. Wilder

The Wilders were friendly folks and enjoyed outings with their Ozark neighbors. In 1908, they visited Williams Cave with the Quigleys. Laura, Almanzo, and their first dog, Shep, are seated at left.

Laura posed with one of Almanzo's farm horses on Rocky Ridge. Both the Wilders liked horseback riding through the Ozark hills.

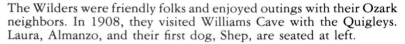

Laura *(left)* and Rose at the edge of the brook in the deep ravine behind the house on Rocky Ridge Farm, during the summer of 1911.

During the early 1900s, the Wilders lived in a little frame house on the edge of Mansfield while they were building up the farm and home at Rocky Ridge. Laura posed on the porch of their house in town, but wrote on the back of the picture: "Just as I am, without one plea," a line from an old hymn.

Laura around 1900, in the ravine on the farm. She is wearing the hand-sewn white dress she made from material that cost ten cents a yard.

"Mrs. Wilder is a woman of delightful personality," noted a neighbor, when asked to describe Laura for the *Missouri Ruralist* feature "Let's Visit Mrs. Wilder," published in 1918.

Laura said: "I wrote when I was doing everything else—my housework and taking care of chickens and cows . . ." Here she is, picking garden peas for supper.

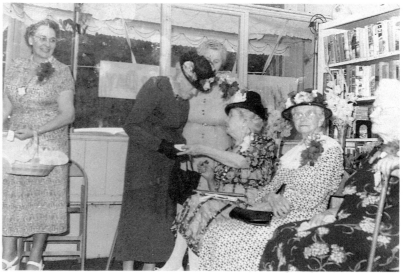

On August 2, 1950, Laura Ingalls Wilder Day was held in Hartville, Missouri. Laura is surrounded by fellow founder members of the Athenians. Seated next to Laura are her longtime friends Emma Frink and Melissa Wilson.

Almanzo and Laura Wilder had been married for sixty-three years when they were photographed in the yard at Rocky Ridge in 1948. Almanzo was ninety-two when he died the following year.

Laura Ingalls Wilder

On September 28, 1951, the people of Mansfield dedicated their branch of the Wright County Library as the Laura Ingalls Wilder Library. The ceremonies were held at the Mansfield High School and at the newly named library. "I cannot tell you how much I value your friendship and how much I appreciate the honor you have bestowed upon me," Laura told the crowd that gathered.

"It was difficult to believe that she was 84 years old," noted the Springfield *News and Leader* at the library dedication. "She was a striking, charming little woman . . . her white hair was piled high and held in place by a gold comb that matched her large ear rings. She wore a beautiful, very dark red, velvet dress. . . ."

When Rose returned to live on her parents' Rocky Ridge Farm in 1928 after several years spent abroad, she built them a new house as a gift. The English-style rock house was constructed in a picturesque setting on the farm, across the ridge from the old frame farmhouse. From 1928 to 1936, Almanzo and Laura lived in the new house, while Rose used the original family homestead as her writing studio and residence. When Rose established a home in Danbury, Connecticut, the Wilders moved back to their old house. "We got homesick," Laura explained. The rock house still stands on a remote corner of Rocky Ridge Farm.

Laura opened the door, soon after moving to the new house at Christmastime 1928. The *Mansfield Mirror* of January 3, 1929, noted that: "Rose Wilder Lane, author and globe-trotter of national fame, has designed and built this beautiful home for her parents. . . . The house is of rock . . . with low eaves and several gables. It has small, paned, plate glass casement windows and frame and tile sills. The house is strictly modern, furnace heated, with electric light and power. They are proud of this beautiful place so near Mansfield. . . . ''

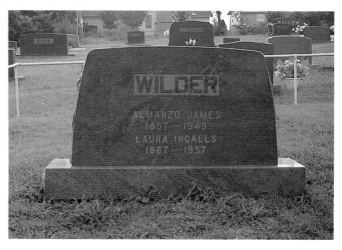

The Mansfield Cemetery is the last resting place of Laura, Almanzo, and Rose Wilder.

CHAPTER 12

Laura's Rose

Rose Wilder spent her final year of school in Crowley, Louisiana, where she lived with her aunt, Eliza Jane Wilder Thayer. At the 1904 Crowley High School graduating exercises, Rose addressed the class with an original poem she composed in Latin.

While growing up in the Missouri Ozarks, Rose Wilder had a pet donkey named Spookendyke. "He was a stubborn, fat little beast who liked to slump his ears and neck and shoulders suddenly when going downhill, and tumble me off over his head."

As a world-renowned author and journalist, Rose Wilder Lane crisscrossed the globe during the 1920s. Her experiences abroad inspired many books and magazine articles for the American media. This photo shows Rose on a walking tour of France in 1921. Later, she traveled and lived in Albania, which provided background for her favorite book, *Peaks of Shala*.

Rose is driving the 1923 blue Buick, which she presented to her parents as a gift. She taught both Laura and Almanzo to drive the car they named Isabelle. Isabelle traveled to California in 1925 and to South Dakota in 1931.

On her 1915 visit to San Francisco to visit Rose and her husband, Gillette Lane, Laura did much sight-seeing. On October 31, she posed with Gillette in the Muir Woods. The Lanes were divorced three years later; Rose never remarried.

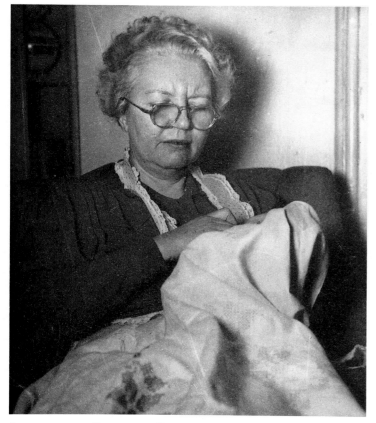

The house at 1018 Vallejo Street in San Francisco still commands a majestic view of the City by the Bay, just as it did when Laura visited Rose and Gillette there in 1915. The visit is described in *West from Home,* based on the letters Laura wrote to Almanzo during her California trip.

An expert needlewoman, Rose wrote two magazine series and a book on the history of American needlework. Photographer Russell Ogg caught her sewing in her New York apartment in 1939.

Rose Wilder Lane

CHAPTER 13

Almanzo and Malone

The *Farmer Boy* house is currently being restored to its 1866 condition.

The only Little House book that was not autobiographical was Laura Ingalls Wilder's *Farmer Boy,* published in 1933. In *Farmer Boy,* Laura described the Yankee youth of Almanzo Wilder on a prosperous farm near Malone, New York, in 1866.

Almanzo's parents, James and Angeline Day Wilder, settled on their farm along the Trout River soon after their marriage in 1843. There six children were born: Laura, Royal, Eliza Jane, Alice, Almanzo, and Perley. Not mentioned in *Farmer Boy* were the oldest and youngest Wilder children. Laura Ingalls Wilder deleted Almanzo's sister Laura from the story because of the confusion that would result from two Lauras in one series of books; Almanzo's youngest brother Perley was not born until three years after the events related in *Farmer Boy.*

Laura Ingalls Wilder never saw Malone, nor the farm where her husband spent his childhood. Almanzo never revisited his boyhood home after moving west as a young man, but his memory was keen and he readily supplied his wife with story material when she was writing *Farmer Boy.*

After the book was published, readers inquired about the setting and Laura was happy to report that "the old house is still standing just as it was when his mother sat at her spinning wheel in the attic chamber." In 1949, Frances and Dorothy Smith, Almanzo's remaining cousins in Malone, found the exact location of the old Wilder farmhouse. Visitors have sought it out ever since.

Since 1966, a marker has designated the birthplace and early home of Almanzo Wilder.

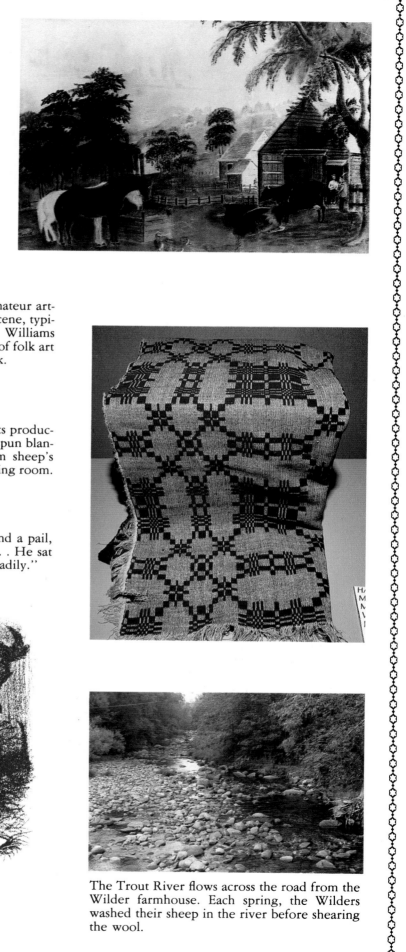

Almanzo's aunt, Sarah Wilder Day, was an amateur artist. As a young woman she painted this farm scene, typical of the Malone region. When artist Garth Williams illustrated *Farmer Boy* he utilized this example of folk art and adapted it for the back jacket of the book.

The Wilder farm was almost self-sufficient in its productiveness when Almanzo was a boy. This homespun blanket was made by Angeline Day Wilder from sheep's wool and it was woven on the loom in her sewing room.

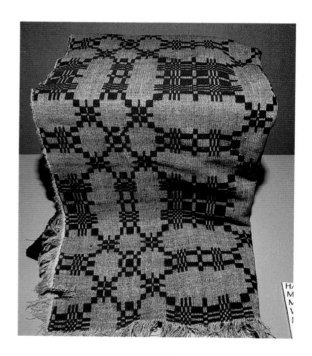

"Almanzo took his own little milking-stool, and a pail, and sat down in Blossom's stall to milk her. . . . He sat with the pail between his feet, and milked steadily."

The Trout River flows across the road from the Wilder farmhouse. Each spring, the Wilders washed their sheep in the river before shearing the wool.

The Wilder family was photographed in Malone during the 1870s, before their move west to Spring Valley, Minnesota. Seated are Royal, Father Wilder, Perley, Mother Wilder, and Alice. Standing are Almanzo, Laura, and Eliza Jane.

Laura Ingalls Wilder explained Almanzo's family's move from Malone to Spring Valley in 1875: "Al- manzo's father had a friend who moved from New York to Eastern Minnesota. He liked it there and Mr. Wilder went out to visit him and look the place over. Mr. Wilder liked it so well that he bought a farm near Spring Valley. The Wilder family moved to the new farm, all the family except Royal and Almanzo, who stayed behind and ran the old farm for a year."

From Spring Valley, three of the Wilders went farther west: In 1879, Royal, Almanzo, and their sister Eliza Jane moved to Dakota Territory to homestead. Eliza Jane became one of the first teachers in the town of De Smet, where she and her brothers located. Their journey to Dakota Terri- tory is recounted in Rose Wilder Lane's novel, *Free Land.*

Before they moved west to Minnesota, Almanzo's sisters and brother studied at the Franklin Academy in Malone, as described in *Farmer Boy.* This stone structure served from 1836 to 1868.

The commodious Wilder home in Spring Valley housed the Wilders until Almanzo's parents moved to Louisiana in 1898. Almanzo spent part of his youth here: In 1890, he and Laura and Rose had lived here. The house was razed in the 1920s.

Almanzo lived long and heartily. In 1943, *The Horn Book Magazine* said of him: "The youngest Wilder is eighty-six now. His hair is not yet gray and he wears glasses only to read fine print."

Almanzo always preferred the Morgan horse to all other breeds. At the first fair held in De Smet, Almanzo and Laura were seated in his buggy at the right of the tent.

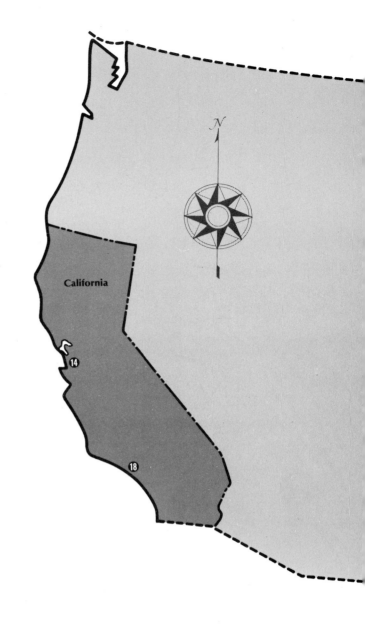

1. **Cuba, New York,** birthplace of Charles Ingalls.

2. **Brookfield, Wisconsin,** birthplace of Caroline Quiner Ingalls.

3. **Concord, Wisconsin,** marriage site and early home of Charles and Caroline Ingalls.

4. **Pepin, Wisconsin,** site of *Little House in the Big Woods;* for information, write Laura Ingalls Wilder Memorial Society, Pepin, WI 54759.

5. **Independence, Kansas,** is thirteen miles from the site of *Little House on the Prairie.* For information, write Little House on the Prairie, Box 110, Independence, KS 67301.

6. **Walnut Grove, Minnesota,** is the site of *On the Banks of Plum Creek.* For information, write Laura Ingalls Wilder Museum, Box 58, Walnut Grove, MN 56180.

7. **Burr Oak, Iowa,** was the home of the Ingalls family from 1876 through 1877. For information, write Laura Ingalls Wilder Park and Museum, Burr Oak, IA 52131.

8. **De Smet, South Dakota,** is the *Little Town on the Prairie* site; for information, write Laura Ingalls Wilder Memorial Society, Box 344, De Smet, SD 57231.

9. **Vinton, Iowa,** is where Mary Ingalls studied at the Iowa College for the Blind from 1881 through 1889. The school is now called the Iowa Braille and Sight Saving School.

10. **Westville, Florida,** was the home of Almanzo, Laura, and Rose Wilder from 1891 through 1892.

11. **Mansfield, Missouri,** is the site of Rocky Ridge Farm, final home of Almanzo and Laura Wilder; for information, write Laura Ingalls Wilder Home and Museum, Route 1, Box 24, Mansfield, MO 65704.

12. **Keystone, South Dakota,** at the foot of Mount Rushmore, was the last home of Mary and Carrie Ingalls. A Carrie Ingalls historic marker stands next to the post office.

13. **Malone, New York,** is the site of *Farmer Boy;* for information, write Laura and Almanzo Wilder Association, Box 283, Malone, NY 12953.

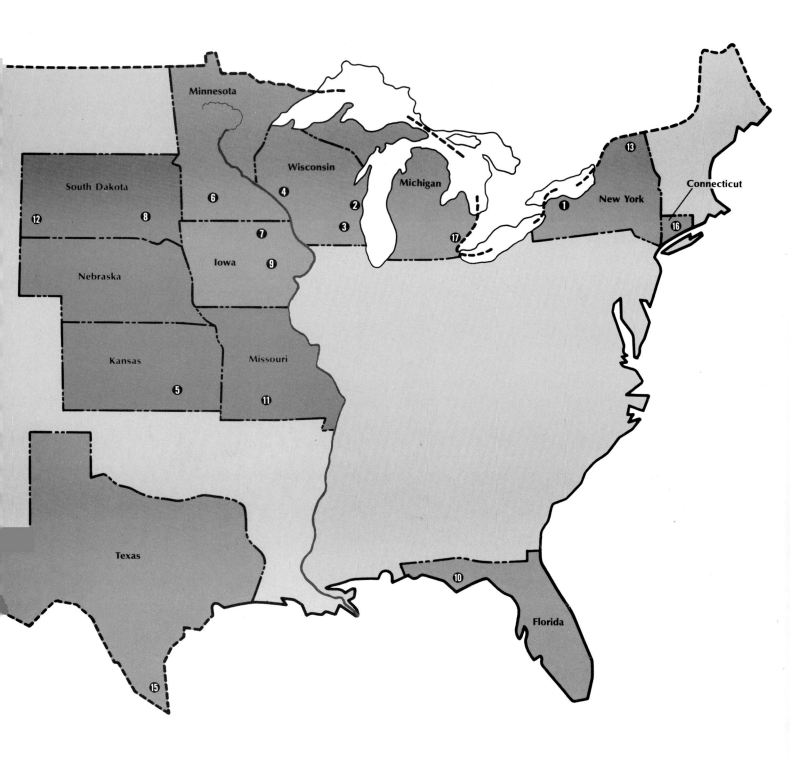

14. San Francisco, California, is the site of *West from Home.* Rose Wilder Lane's home still stands at 1018 Vallejo Street.

15. Harlingen, Texas, was the home of Rose Wilder Lane from 1965 through 1968.

16. Danbury, Connecticut, was the home of Rose Wilder Lane from 1938 through 1968. Her home is located at 23 King Street.

17. Detroit, Michigan, named a Laura Ingalls Wilder Library, the first in the world, in 1949. It is located on Seven Mile and Rogge. A collection of Wilder manuscripts and memorabilia is housed in the Rare Book Room of the main library.

18. Pomona, California, named a Laura Ingalls Wilder Room in its public library in 1950. On permanent exhibit is a collection of manuscript material and memorabilia.

LAURA'S READERS STILL VISIT

After her Little House books became famous, Laura Ingalls Wilder was constantly visited by readers of her stories. During the summer months, a steady trickle of cars arrived at Rocky Ridge Farm, bearing children and parents who wanted to meet their favorite writer. Following Laura's death in 1957, the house on Rocky Ridge Farm became a memorial to the Wilders, preserved as they left it. Since then, many other sites connected with the Ingalls-Wilder families have joined the Little House sites. The following directory lists the places that preserve "the real things" Laura Ingalls Wilder wrote about:

Laura Ingalls Wilder Memorial Society, Box 269, Pepin, WI 54759
Little House on the Prairie Site, Box 110, Independence, KS 67301
Laura and Almanzo Wilder Association, Box 283, Malone, NY 12953
Laura Ingalls Wilder Museum, Box 58, Walnut Grove, MN 56180
Laura Ingalls Wilder Park and Museum, Box 354, Burr Oak, IA 52131
Laura Ingalls Wilder Site, 909 South Broadway, Spring Valley, MN 55975
Laura Ingalls Wilder Memorial Society, Box 344, De Smet, SD 57231
Laura Ingalls Wilder Home and Museum, Route 1, Box 24, Mansfield, MO 65704

When writing these sites for information, please include a postage stamp with your request.

A Laura Ingalls Wilder Chronology

1836 JANUARY 10
Charles Phillip Ingalls born in Cuba, New York.

1839 DECEMBER 12
Caroline Lake Quiner born in Milwaukee County, Wisconsin.

1857 FEBRUARY 13
Almanzo James Wilder born near Malone, New York.

1860 FEBRUARY 1
Charles Ingalls and Caroline Quiner married in Concord, Wisconsin.

1863 SEPTEMBER 23
Charles Ingalls purchased Pepin County farm.

1865 JANUARY 10
Mary Amelia Ingalls born in Pepin, Wisconsin.

1867 FEBRUARY 7
Laura Elizabeth Ingalls born in Pepin.

1869
The Ingalls family moved to Kansas.

1870 AUGUST 3
Caroline Celestia (Carrie) Ingalls born in Montgomery County, Kansas.

1871
The Ingalls family returned to their Pepin farm.

1874
The Ingalls family moved to Walnut Grove, Minnesota.

1875 NOVEMBER 1
Charles Frederick Ingalls born in Walnut Grove.

1876 AUGUST 27
Charles Frederick Ingalls died; buried in South Troy, Minnesota.

1876–1877
The Ingalls family lived in Burr Oak, Iowa.

1877 MAY 23
Grace Pearl Ingalls born in Burr Oak.

1878–1879
The Ingalls family lived in Walnut Grove.

1879
The Ingalls family moved to Dakota Territory.

1885 AUGUST 25
Laura Ingalls and Almanzo Wilder married in De Smet, South Dakota.

1886 DECEMBER 5
Rose Wilder born in De Smet.

1889 AUGUST
Infant son of Laura and Almanzo was born and died in De Smet.

1894
Laura, Almanzo, and Rose Wilder settle in Mansfield, Missouri.

1901 OCTOBER 16
Grace Ingalls and Nate Dow married in De Smet.

1902 JUNE 8
Charles Ingalls died in De Smet.

1904
Rose Wilder graduated from Crowley (Louisiana) High School.

1909 MARCH 24
Rose Wilder married Claire Gillette Lane in San Francisco.

1911
Laura published her first *Missouri Ruralist* contribution.
Rose Wilder Lane's only child, a son, was born and died.

1912   AUGUST 1
Carrie Ingalls married David Swanzey in Rapid City, South Dakota.

1918
Rose and Gillette Lane divorced.

1920–1923
Rose Wilder Lane traveled in Europe and the Near East.

1924   APRIL 20
Caroline Ingalls died in De Smet.

1928   OCTOBER 17
Mary Ingalls died at the home of Carrie, in Keystone, South Dakota.

1932
Little House in the Big Woods published.

1933
Laura's *Farmer Boy* and Rose's *Let the Hurricane Roar* published.

1935
Little House on the Prairie published.

1937
On the Banks of Plum Creek published.

1938
Laura and Almanzo visited the Pacific Coast and returned to De Smet.

1939
By the Shores of Silver Lake published.

1940
The Long Winter published.

1941   NOVEMBER 10
Grace Ingalls Dow died in Manchester, South Dakota.
Little Town on the Prairie published.

1943
These Happy Golden Years published.

1946   JUNE 2
Carrie Ingalls Swanzey died in Rapid City, South Dakota.

1949   OCTOBER 23
Almanzo Wilder died at Rocky Ridge Farm.

1954
Laura Ingalls Wilder Award established by the American Library Association with Laura as first recipient.

1957   FEBRUARY 10
Laura Ingalls Wilder died at Rocky Ridge Farm.

1968   OCTOBER 30
Rose Wilder Lane died in Danbury, Connecticut.

Illustration Credits

The mix of contemporary, historic, and artistic illustrations that comprise this book has been gathered from a variety of sources. All of the color photography, unless otherwise indicated, is the work of Leslie A. Kelly. Illustrations by Helen Sewell and Mildred Boyle and illustrations by Garth Williams for the first and second editions of the Little House books are reproduced courtesy of Harper Junior Books.

The historic photographs are the property of several of the Laura Ingalls Wilder historic sites. A sincere thanks is offered for the use of these valuable materials. The following index lists sources for these photographs.

PAGE 20, Pa and Ma, Laura Ingalls Wilder Home Association, Mansfield, Missouri (hereafter referred to as LIWHA); Ingalls family, courtesy of Rex Phillips family.

PAGE 22, Huleatt children, LIWHA.

PAGE 23, Pepin school, Laura Ingalls Wilder Memorial Society, Pepin, Wisconsin.

PAGE 30, Family Bible, LIWHA.

PAGE 31, Osage Indian, courtesy of Oklahoma Historical Society.

PAGE 35, Plum Creek, 1947, courtesy of Garth Williams.

PAGE 39, Nelson family, courtesy of Wilder Museum, Walnut Grove, Minnesota; map, LIWHA.

PAGE 43, Jewel box, LIWHA.

PAGE 46, Historic hotel photograph, courtesy of Laura Ingalls Wilder Park and Museum, Burr Oak, Iowa; kitchen, Laura Ingalls Wilder Park and Museum.

PAGE 49, School and church, Laura Ingalls Wilder Park and Museum; Grace, LIWHA.

PAGE 53, China figure, William Anderson photograph.

PAGE 56, Photographs courtesy of Garth Williams.

PAGE 59, Historic store photograph from the Aubrey Sherwood Collection.

PAGE 60, Manuscript, courtesy of the Rare Book and Gift Room, Detroit Public Library; Youth's Companion, William Anderson Collection; snowbound train, Laura Ingalls Wilder Memorial Society, De Smet, South Dakota (hereafter referred to as LIWMS).

PAGE 61, Ingalls sisters, LIWHA; Pa and Ma, LIWMS.

PAGE 65, Map and Main Street from the Aubrey Sherwood Collection.

PAGE 66, Map, courtesy of Herbert Hoover Presidential Library, West Branch, Iowa (hereafter referred to as HHPL); name card, Rex Phillips family; book title page, courtesy of the Rare Book and Gift Room, Detroit Public Library.

PAGE 67, Aubrey Sherwood Collection.

PAGE 68, Dunn paintings, courtesy of the South Dakota Art Museum, Brookings.

PAGE 70, Photograph courtesy of Garth Williams.

PAGE 73, Laura and Almanzo, LIWHA.

PAGE 75, Laura and Almanzo, Rose, LIWHA; wedding announcement courtesy of the De Smet News, De Smet, South Dakota.

PAGE 78, Upper left photograph by Ron Nelson.

PAGE 81, Ingalls family, LIWMS; Third Street, LIWMS.

PAGE 82, Both photographs of Mary, LIWMS; letter, William Anderson Collection.

PAGE 83, All historic photographs, LIWMS; marker photograph by William Anderson.

PAGE 84, Grace, LIWMS; Grace and Nate, HHPL; farm, William Anderson Collection.

PAGE 85, Laura's artwork, LIWHA.

PAGE 86, Laura and Almanzo, LIWHA.

PAGE 87, Laura and Almanzo, HHPL.

PAGE 88, Laura's painting, LIWHA.

PAGE 92, Cattle photographs by William Anderson.

PAGE 97, Mansfield and fence scene, LIWHA.

PAGE 98, Wilder home, HHPL; yard scene, William Anderson Collection.

PAGE 99, House interiors, HHPL.

PAGE 100, Cabinets, HHPL; barn, LIWHA.

PAGE 101, Kitchen, HHPL.

PAGE 102, Almanzo and outbuilding, HHPL.

PAGE 103, Almanzo and barn, LIWHA.

PAGE 104, All photographs, LIWHA.

PAGE 105, All photographs, LIWHA.

PAGE 106, Laura at the library, LIWHA.

PAGE 107, Historic photograph of house, LIWHA.

PAGE 108, Rose at graduation, HHPL; Rose and donkey, LIWHA; Rose on walking tour, LIWMS.

PAGE 109, Rose in car, Laura and Gillette, HHPL; Rose sewing, courtesy of Russell Ogg; San Francisco house, William Anderson photograph.

PAGES 110-111, Wilder house, marker, Trout River, William Anderson photographs.

PAGE 111, Sarah Wilder Day painting, courtesy of Almanzo and Laura Wilder Association, Malone, New York.

PAGE 112, Wilder family, LIWHA; Eliza Jane, courtesy of Franklin County Historical Society, Malone, New York.

PAGE 113, Franklin Academy, courtesy of Franklin County Historical Society, Malone, New York; Wilder house, courtesy of Bettie Thayer Huey; Wilders in buggy, LIWHA.